Mornings with
JESUS

A JOURNAL

Guideposts
New York, New York

Mornings with Jesus Journal

ISBN-10: 0-8249-3177-7
ISBN-13: 978-0-8249-3177-3

Published by Guideposts
16 East 34th Street
New York, New York 10016
Guideposts.org

Acknowledgments
Every attempt has been made to credit the sources of copyrighted material used in this book. If any such acknowledgment has been inadvertently omitted or miscredited, receipt of such information would be appreciated.

Scripture quotations marked (ESV) are taken from the Holy Bible, English Standard Version, copyright © 2001 by Crossway Bibles, a division of Good News Publishers. Used by permission. All rights reserved.

Scripture quotations marked (MSG) are taken from *The Message*. Copyright © 1993, 1994, 1995, 1996, 2000, 2001, 2002 by Eugene H. Peterson.

Scripture quotations marked (NAS) are taken from the *New American Standard Bible,* copyright © 1960, 1962, 1963, 1968, 1971, 1972, 1973, 1975, 1977, 1995 by the Lockman Foundation. Used by permission. www.Lockman.org

Scripture quotations marked (NIV) are taken from *The Holy Bible, New International Version, NIV.* Copyright © 1973, 1978, 1984, 2011 by Biblica. All rights reserved worldwide.

Scripture quotations marked (NKJV) are taken from *The Holy Bible, New King James Version.* Copyright © 1997, 1990, 1985, 1983 by Thomas Nelson, Inc.

Scripture quotations marked (NLT) are taken from the *Holy Bible,* New Living Translation. Copyright © 1996. Used by permission of Tyndale House Publishers, Inc., Wheaton, Illinois 60189. All rights reserved.

Cover and interior by Lookout Design, Inc.
Typeset by Aptara

Printed and bound in China
10 9 8 7 6 5 4 3 2 1

Introduction

IN THE HURRIEDNESS OF OUR LIVES, we can often miss the wisdom, truth, compassion, kindness and gentleness of Jesus' teachings. This special new journal, *Mornings with Jesus*, will help you draw closer to the heart of Jesus by spending time in His presence and comfort. Discover all of the wonderful treasures of His words and what they reveal through your own writings and reflections.

Record your thoughts and feelings in these beautiful pages. You can even bring this journal with you and update it throughout the day with the promises, victories and insights of His way.

Walk alongside Jesus. Spend time in His presence. Go to Him. Listen to Him. Let go of worry and write *of*—and *to*—Him here.

The Word *became flesh and made his dwelling among us.*
We have seen his glory, the glory of the one and only Son,
who came from the Father, full of grace and truth.

—JOHN 1:14 (NIV)

*T*herefore do not be anxious, saying, "What shall we eat?" or
"What shall we drink?" or "What shall we wear?" For
the Gentiles seek after all these things, and your heavenly Father
knows that you need them all. But seek first the kingdom of God and
his righteousness, and all these things will be added to you.

—MATTHEW 6:31–33 (ESV)

Blessed are the poor in spirit,
for theirs is the kingdom of heaven.
—MATTHEW 5:3 (ESV)

By this we know that we abide in him and he in us,

because he has given us of his Spirit.

—1 JOHN **4 : 1 3** (ESV)

If we confess our sins, He is faithful and righteous to forgive us our sins and to cleanse us from all unrighteousness.

—1 JOHN 1:9 (NAS)

*Rejoice always; pray without ceasing; in everything give thanks;
for this is God's will for you in Christ Jesus.*

—1 THESSALONIANS 5:16–18 (NAS)

Surely he took up our pain and bore our suffering, yet we considered him punished by God, stricken by him, and afflicted.

—ISAIAH 53 : 4 (NIV)

Whatever you do, work at it with all your heart, as working for the Lord, not for human masters, since you know that you will receive an inheritance from the Lord as a reward. It is the Lord Christ you are serving.

—COLOSSIANS 3: 2 3–2 4 (NIV)

Blessed are those who mourn, for they shall be comforted.
—MATTHEW 5:4 (ESV)

Bear with each other and forgive one another if any of you has a grievance against someone. Forgive as the Lord forgave you. And over all these virtues put on love, which binds them all together in perfect unity. Let the peace of Christ rule in your hearts, since as members of one body you were called to peace. And be thankful.

—COLOSSIANS 3: 1 3 — 1 5 (NIV)

Follow God's example, therefore, as dearly loved children and walk in the way of love, just as Christ loved us and gave himself up for us as a fragrant offering and sacrifice to God.

—EPHESIANS 5:1–2 (NIV)

He tends his flock like a shepherd: He gathers the lambs
in his arms and carries them close to his heart;
he gently leads those that have young.

—ISAIAH 40 : 11 (NIV)

For we do not have a high priest who is unable to empathize with
our weaknesses, but we have one who has been tempted
in every way, just as we are—yet he did not sin.

—HEBREWS 4: 1 5 (NIV)

Peace I leave with you; my peace I give you.
I do not give to you as the world gives. Do not let your hearts
be troubled and do not be afraid.

—JOHN 14 : 27 (NIV)

Greater love has no one than this: to lay down one's life for one's friends.

—JOHN 15:13 (NIV)

*For to us a child is born, to us a son is given, and
the government will be on his shoulders.
And he will be called Wonderful Counselor, Mighty God,
Everlasting Father, Prince of Peace. Of the greatness of
his government and peace there will be no end.*

—ISAIAH 9:6—7 (NIV)

*In the beginning was the Word, and the Word was with God,
and the Word was God.*

—JOHN 1:1 (NIV)

S - 1

Bt - 3

A - - 3

A - 1

B - - 3

No one lights a lamp and puts it in a place where it will be hidden, or under a bowl. Instead they put it on its stand, so that those who come in may see the light.

—LUKE 11 : 33 (NIV)

And calling the crowd to him with his disciples, he said to them, "If anyone would come after me, let him deny himself and take up his cross and follow me. For whoever would save his life will lose it, but whoever loses his life for my sake and the gospel's will save it."

—MARK 8:34–35 (ESV)

Do nothing from selfish ambition or conceit, but in humility count others more significant than yourselves. Let each of you look not only to his own interests, but also to the interests of others. Have this mind among yourselves, which is yours in Christ Jesus....

—PHILIPPIANS 2:3–5 (ESV)

Blessed are those who hunger and thirst for righteousness,
for they shall be satisfied.
—MATTHEW 5:6 (ESV)

Who is to condemn? Christ Jesus is the one who died—more than that,
who was raised—who is at the right hand of God, who indeed is interceding for us.
—ROMANS 8:34 (ESV)

Be still before the Lord and wait patiently for him....
—PSALM 37 : 7 (NIV)

The whole town gathered at the door, and Jesus healed many who had various diseases. He also drove out many demons, but he would not let the demons speak because they knew who he was.

—MARK 1:33-34 (NIV)

For to me, to live is Christ and to die is gain.
—PHILIPPIANS 1 : 2 1 (NIV)

Therefore everyone who hears these words of mine and puts them into practice is like a wise man who built his house on the rock. The rain came down, the streams rose, and the winds blew and beat against that house; yet it did not fall, because it had its foundation on the rock.

—MATTHEW 7:24–25 (NIV)

He will be great and will be called the Son of the Most High.

—LUKE 1:32 (NIV)

What shall we say the kingdom of God is like, or what parable
shall we use to describe it? It is like a mustard seed, which is the
smallest of all seeds on earth. Yet when planted, it grows and becomes
the largest of all garden plants, with such big branches that
the birds can perch in its shade.

—MARK 4:30–32 (NIV)

Blessed are the pure in heart, for they shall see God.

—MATTHEW 5:8 (ESV)

Blessed are the merciful, for they shall receive mercy.

—MATTHEW 5 : 7 (ESV)

Ask and it will be given to you; seek and you will find; knock and the door will be opened to you. For everyone who asks receives; the one who seeks finds; and to the one who knocks, the door will be opened.

—MATTHEW 7:7–8 (NIV)

When evening came, many who were demon-possessed were brought
to him, and he drove out the spirits with a word and healed all the
sick. This was to fulfill what was spoken through the prophet Isaiah:
"He took up our infirmities and bore our diseases."

—MATTHEW 8:16–17 (NIV)

On hearing this, Jesus said, "It is not the healthy who need a doctor, but the sick. But go and learn what this means: 'I desire mercy, not sacrifice.' For I have not come to call the righteous, but sinners."

—MATTHEW 9:12–13 (NIV)

Let the words of my mouth and the meditation of my heart be acceptable in your sight, O Lord, my rock and my redeemer.

—PSALM 19:14 (ESV)

We were therefore buried with him through baptism into death in order that, just as Christ was raised from the dead through the glory of the Father, we too may live a new life.

—ROMANS 6:4 (NIV)

I am the good shepherd. The good shepherd
lays down his life for the sheep.

—JOHN 10:11 (NIV)

They took palm branches and went out to meet him, shouting,
"Hosanna! Blessed is he who comes in the name of the Lord!
Blessed is the king of Israel!"

—JOHN 12:13 (NIV)

Whoever serves me must follow me; and where I am, my servant also will be. My Father will honor the one who serves me.

—JOHN 12:26 (NIV)

*O*n the last day of the feast, the great day, Jesus stood up and cried out,

"If anyone thirsts, let him come to me and drink."

—JOHN 7:37 (ESV)

Let not your hearts be troubled.
Believe in God; believe also in me.

—JOHN 14 : 1 (ESV)

Thomas said to him, "Lord, we do not know where you are going. How can we know the way?" Jesus said to him, "I am the way, and the truth, and the life. No one comes to the Father except through me."

—JOHN 14:5–6 (ESV)

Abide in me, and I in you. As the branch cannot bear fruit by itself, unless it abides in the vine, neither can you, unless you abide in me. I am the vine; you are the branches. Whoever abides in me and I in him, he it is that bears much fruit, for apart from me you can do nothing.

—JOHN 15:4–5 (ESV)

Jesus answered, "My kingdom is not of this world. If my kingdom were of this world, my servants would have been fighting, that I might not be delivered over to the Jews. But my kingdom is not from the world."

—JOHN 18:36 (ESV)

For God so loved the world, that he gave his only Son, that whoever believes in him should not perish but have eternal life. For God did not send his Son into the world to condemn the world, but in order that the world might be saved through him. Whoever believes in him is not condemned, but whoever does not believe is condemned already, because he has not believed in the name of the only Son of God.

—JOHN 3:16–18 (ESV)

My sheep listen to my voice; I know them, and they follow me.
I give them eternal life, and they shall never perish;
no one will snatch them out of my hand.

—JOHN 10:27–28 (NIV)

*J*esus said to them, "I am the bread of life; whoever comes to me shall not hunger, and whoever believes in me shall never thirst."

—JOHN 6:35 (ESV)

For everyone who exalts himself will be humbled, and he who humbles himself will be exalted.

—LUKE 14 : 11 (ESV)

Indeed, it is easier for a camel to go through the eye of a needle than for someone who is rich to enter the kingdom of God.

—LUKE 18:25 (NIV)

et the news about him spread all the more, so that crowds of people came to hear him and to be healed of their sicknesses. But Jesus often withdrew to lonely places and prayed.

—LUKE 5: 1 5 — 1 6 (NIV)

Haven't you read this passage of Scripture: "'The stone the builders rejected has become the cornerstone; the Lord has done this, and it is marvelous in our eyes'?"

—MARK 12:10–11 (NIV)

As Jesus looked up, he saw the rich putting their gifts into the temple treasury. He also saw a poor widow put in two very small copper coins. "Truly I tell you," he said, "this poor widow has put in more than all the others. All these people gave their gifts out of their wealth; but she out of her poverty put in all she had to live on."

—LUKE 21 : 1–4 (NIV)

Blessed are the peacemakers,
for they shall be called sons of God.
—MATTHEW 5: 9 (ESV)

Come to Me, all you who labor and are heavy laden, and I will give you rest. Take My yoke upon you and learn from Me, for I am gentle and lowly in heart, and you will find rest for your souls.

For My yoke is easy and My burden is light.

—MATTHEW 11 : 28 – 30 (NKJV)

esus answered and said to them, "Go and tell John the things which you hear and see: The blind see and the lame walk; the lepers are cleansed and the deaf hear; the dead are raised up and the poor have the gospel preached to them."

—MATTHEW 11 : 4–5 (NKJV)

hen Jesus said to His disciples, "If anyone desires to come after Me, let him deny himself, and take up his cross, and follow Me. For whoever desires to save his life will lose it, but whoever loses his life for My sake will find it."

—MATTHEW 16:24–25 (NKJV)

Very early in the morning, while it was still dark, Jesus got up, left the house and went off to a solitary place, where he prayed.

—MARK 1:35 (NIV)

hen Peter came to Him and said, "Lord, how often shall my brother sin against me, and I forgive him? Up to seven times?" Jesus said to him, "I do not say to you, up to seven times, but up to seventy times seven."

—MATTHEW 18:21–22 (NKJV)

And He called a child to Himself and set him before them, and
said, "Truly I say to you, unless you are converted and become like
children, you will not enter the kingdom of heaven.
Whoever then humbles himself as this child,
he is the greatest in the kingdom of heaven."

—MATTHEW 18:2-4 (NAS)

And Jesus answered and said to them, "Truly I say to you,
if you have faith and do not doubt, you will not only do what
was done to the fig tree, but even if you say to this mountain,
'Be taken up and cast into the sea,' it will happen.
And all things you ask in prayer, believing, you will receive."

—MATTHEW 21:21–22 (NAS)

"You shall love the Lord your God with all your heart, and with all your soul, and with all your mind." This is the great and foremost commandment. The second is like it, "You shall love your neighbor as yourself." On these two commandments depend the whole Law and the Prophets.

—MATTHEW 22:37–40 (NAS)

For I was hungry, and you gave Me something to eat;
I was thirsty, and you gave Me something to drink;
I was a stranger, and you invited Me in.

—MATTHEW 25 : 35 (NAS)

And Jesus came and said to them, *"All authority in heaven and on earth has been given to me. Go therefore and make disciples of all nations, baptizing them in the name of the Father and of the Son and of the Holy Spirit, teaching them to observe all that I have commanded you. And behold, I am with you always, to the end of the age."*

—MATTHEW 28:18–20 (ESV)

And when Jesus was baptized, immediately he went up from the water, and behold, the heavens were opened to him, and he saw the Spirit of God descending like a dove and coming to rest on him; and behold, a voice from heaven said, "This is my beloved Son, with whom I am well pleased."

—MATTHEW 3:16–17 (ESV)

While walking by the Sea of Galilee, he saw two brothers, Simon (who is called Peter) and Andrew his brother, casting a net into the sea, for they were fishermen. And he said to them, "Follow me, and I will make you fishers of men." Immediately they left their nets and followed him.

—MATTHEW 4: 1 8 – 2 0 (ESV)

Then Jesus spoke to them again, saying, "I am the light of the world. He who follows Me shall not walk in darkness, but have the light of life."

—JOHN 8:12 (NKJV)

Therefore, if anyone is in Christ, he is a new creation.
The old has passed away; behold, the new has come.

—2 CORINTHIANS 5:17 (ESV)

Blessed are the meek, for they shall inherit the earth.
—MATTHEW 5: 5 (ESV)

*J*umping out of the boat, Peter walked on the water to Jesus. But
when he looked down at the waves churning beneath his feet,
he lost his nerve and started to sink. He cried, "Master, save me!"
Jesus didn't hesitate. He reached down and grabbed his hand.
Then he said, "Faint-heart, what got into you?"

—MATTHEW 14:29–31 (MSG)

Therefore God exalted him to the highest place and gave him the name that is above every name, that at the name of Jesus every knee should bow, in heaven and on earth and under the earth, and every tongue acknowledge that Jesus Christ is Lord, to the glory of God the Father.

—PHILIPPIANS 2:9–11 (NIV)

Behold, the virgin shall be with child, and bear a Son, and they shall call His name Immanuel," which is translated, "God with us."

—MATTHEW 1:23 (NKJV)

Blessed are those who are persecuted for righteousness' sake,
for theirs is the kingdom of heaven.
—MATTHEW 5:10 (ESV)

You have heard that it was said, "You shall love your neighbor and hate your enemy." But I say to you, love your enemies and pray for those who persecute you.

—MATTHEW 5:43–44 (ESV)

Give us today our daily bread.
—MATTHEW 6:11 (NIV)

Therefore I tell you, do not worry about your life, what you will eat or drink; or about your body, what you will wear. Is not life more than food, and the body more than clothes? Look at the birds of the air; they do not sow or reap or store away in barns, and yet your heavenly Father feeds them. Are you not much more valuable than they? Can any one of you by worrying add a single hour to your life?

—MATTHEW 6:25–27 (NIV)

You are the salt of the earth. But if the salt loses its saltiness, how can it be made salty again? It is no longer good for anything, except to be thrown out and trampled underfoot. You are the light of the world. A town built on a hill cannot be hidden.

—MATTHEW 5:13–14 (NIV)

Therefore, since we have been justified through faith, we have peace with God through our Lord Jesus Christ.

—ROMANS 5:1 (NIV)

But that you may know that the Son of Man has authority on earth to forgive sins"—he said to the paralytic—"I say to you, rise, pick up your bed, and go home."

—MARK 2: 10–11 (ESV)

And the seeds that fell on the good soil represent honest, good-hearted people who hear God's word, cling to it, and patiently produce a huge harvest.

—LUKE 8:15 (NLT)

A Note from the Editors

WE HOPE YOU ENJOY *Mornings with Jesus Journal*, created by Guideposts Books and Inspirational Media. In all of our books, magazines and outreach efforts, we aim to deliver inspiration and encouragement, help you grow in your faith, and celebrate God's love in every aspect of your daily life.

Thank you for making a difference with your purchase of this book, which helps fund our many outreach programs to the military, prisons, hospitals, nursing homes and schools. To learn more, visit GuidepostsFoundation.org.

We also maintain many useful and uplifting online resources. Visit Guideposts.org to read true stories of hope and inspiration, access OurPrayer network, sign up for free newsletters, join our Facebook community, and follow our stimulating blogs.

To order your favorite Guideposts publications, go to ShopGuideposts.org, call (800) 932-2145 or write to Guideposts, PO Box 5815, Harlan, Iowa 51593.